How To Convince Your Parents You Can...

Care For A Pet Tarantula

Amie Jane Leavitt

Mitchell Lane
PUBLISHERS

P.O. Box 196
Hockessin, Delaware 19707
Visit us on the web: www.mitchelllane.com
Comments? email us: mitchelllane@mitchelllane.com

Mitchell Lane
PUBLISHERS

Printing   2   3   4   5   6   7   8   9

A Robbie Reader/How to Convince Your Parents You Can...

Care for a Pet Bunny	Care for a Pet Mouse
Care for a Pet Chameleon	Care for a Pet Snake
Care for a Pet Chimpanzee	**Care for a Pet Tarantula**
Care for a Pet Ferret	Care for a Potbellied Pig
Care for a Pet Horse	Care for a Wild Pony from Assateague

Library of Congress Cataloging-in-Publication Data
Leavitt, Amie Jane.
  Care for a pet tarantula / by Amie Jane Leavitt.
     p. cm. — (A Robbie reader. How to convince your parents you can)
  Includes bibliographical references and index.
  ISBN-13: 978-1-58415-603-1 (library bound)
  I. Tarantulas as pets—Juvenile literature. I. Title.
  SF459.T37L43 2008
  639'.7—dc22

                                                                        2007000809

ABOUT THE AUTHOR: Amie Jane Leavitt, an accomplished author and photographer, was surprised to discover how fascinating nature's biggest spiders really are. The only unusual pet she ever had was a pair of "kissing fish" while she was in college. Yet, after learning about tarantulas, she can see why people would be interested in having one of these curious creatures for their very own. Amie graduated from Brigham Young University as an education major and since then has taught all subjects and grade levels in both private and public schools. She is an adventurer who loves to travel the globe in search of interesting story ideas and beautiful places to capture on film. She has written dozens of books for kids, has contributed to online and print media, and has worked as a consultant, writer, and editor for numerous educational publishing and assessment companies.

PHOTO CREDITS: All photographs © 2008 JupiterImages Corporation.

TABLE OF CONTENTS

Words in **bold** type can be found in the glossary.

On the prowl. This tarantula is hunting for something to eat.

A PET SPIDER?

So, you want to get a pet, but you think a cat or dog is just too boring? You might think about getting a **tarantula** (tuh-RAN-chuh-luh) instead. Tarantulas are huge spiders. Their bodies and legs are covered with fuzzy hair.

Why would anyone want to have a spider as a pet? Many people are afraid of these eight-legged creatures. They think tarantulas are big, hairy, and mean. They might not be so afraid if they knew all the facts about tarantulas.

It is true that some spiders would not make good pets, but tarantulas are not bad spiders at all. Many people enjoy keeping these animals as pets in their homes. Tarantulas are very gentle animals. They rarely bite, and they would rather run away from danger than attack. They don't make any loud noises. They just like to stay by themselves in their cages.

Long ago, the streets of Taranto, Italy, were crawling with hairy wolf spiders. Tarantulas are named for this city, because the new spiders reminded people of wolf spiders.

Tarantulas are good to have as pets because they are very easy to care for. All you need is a simple cage, a container for water, and some chips of wood for digging.

Tarantulas require little attention. You have to do many things for cats, dogs, and other pets, but you will not have to do as much for a tarantula. You will not have to take your tarantula out for a walk or run and play with it in the backyard. You will not have to train it to use the bathroom outside.

Your parents will be very happy that they don't have to bug you about doing these things for your pet. All you have to do is give your tarantula food and water, and clean its cage sometimes.

Another great thing about tarantulas is that they are so much fun to watch. Some tarantulas like to climb. Others like to jump. Most like to dig holes in the wood or soil and hide. It is fun to watch everything they do.

Yet it is probably not a good idea to hold your tarantula. It could become scared and jump out of your hands, which could hurt or even kill your tarantula. These pets are better left inside their cages. You can just watch them crawl around from a distance.

Before you decide to get a tarantula as a pet, you really need to learn more about them. Where do they live in the wild? What kind of food do they eat? How long will they live? Do they shed their skin like other spiders? What kind of home do they need?

If you want one of these pets, your parents will have to say it is okay. But first, they will probably want to know the answers to these questions. It is best that you learn a lot about tarantulas before you ask to get one. The answers to all these questions and more can be found in the rest of this book.

The goliath bird-eating tarantula is the biggest spider in the tarantula family. If you set it on a dinner plate, it would cover the entire thing.

THE LIFE OF A TARANTULA

There are many different types of tarantulas. The largest one grows as big as a Frisbee. The smallest one is probably just as big as your hand. Baby tarantulas are so small that they can fit inside a pill bottle.

Tarantulas live in many different places all over the world. They are found on every continent except Antarctica. This is the continent on the southernmost part of the earth. It is too cold there for most things to live. Tarantulas like to live in warm places.

Many tarantulas dig burrows, or holes, in the ground. They spend most of their lives in these burrows. Some tarantulas live in trees. They can climb and jump from branch to branch.

Female tarantulas live longer than male tarantulas. Females can live up to thirty years!

Males live only ten years at the most. Female tarantulas are also usually larger than male tarantulas.

Some animals are born only in the springtime. Not tarantulas. Baby tarantulas are born any time of the year.

New babies are made during a time called mating season. Male tarantulas will travel many miles to find a female tarantula during this time. They know where she is because of her scent.

A female tarantula spins a silky **egg sac**. When her babies are big enough, the sac will break . . .

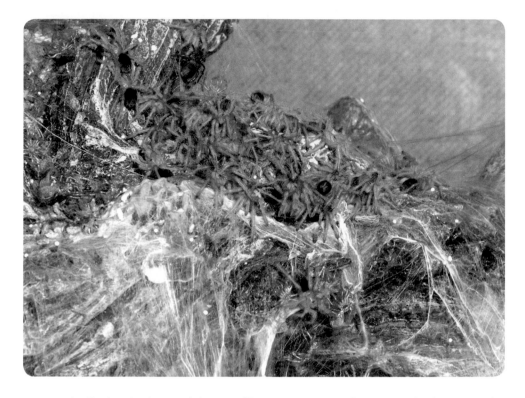

... and all the baby spiders will come scurrying out. A thousand baby tarantulas can fit inside one egg sac.

Male tarantulas have a strong sense of smell. They can smell female tarantulas from very far away.

When a male tarantula finds the burrow of a female tarantula, he does two things. First he makes a tapping sound with his legs. Then he does a little dance. He is trying to make the female like him. He wants her to come out of her house and see him.

Sometimes she will come out right away. Other times he will have to do a lot of dancing for her to

come out. When she does come out, she decides if she likes him or not. If she doesn't like him, she will fight with him. Then she will run back into her hole. The male tarantula still won't go away. He will keep tapping and dancing to see if she will come back out. Male tarantulas do not give up easily.

If the female tarantula does like the male tarantula, she will let him come into her house. The two tarantulas will mate. Then the male will go away. Sometimes the female will eat the male, but, luckily for the males, this doesn't happen very often.

The female tarantula will spin a silky sac for her eggs. This will help keep them safe. She will protect the sac until the babies are born. It takes six to nine weeks for the spiders to hatch from their eggs. The egg sac can hold up to 1,000 eggs. That is a lot of baby tarantulas!

Tarantulas are different from other spiders when it comes to catching their food. They do not spin webs to catch food, but hunt for it instead. Usually they come out of their burrow only at night to hunt. This makes it easier for the tarantula to hide and sneak up on its prey.

Tarantulas are **carnivores** (CAR-nih-vorz). That means that they do not eat plants. They eat other animals for food. Small tarantulas eat insects and other spiders. Large tarantulas eat small snakes, lizards, frogs, mice, birds, and bats. Usually a tarantula will not eat something much bigger than itself.

A showdown at the tarantula corral. Who do you think will win, the spider or the fly?

The Chilean rose tarantula is one of the best kinds of spiders to get as a pet. It is small, easy to take care of, and inexpensive to buy.

 Chapter Three **3**

A TRIP TO THE PET STORE

You can buy tarantulas at many pet stores. There are certain things you should look for when buying this kind of pet.

First, ask the store's owner which ones are male and which are female. You will want to buy a female tarantula, because females live much longer than males. Males will also want to get out of the cage all the time to find females tarantulas. This makes male tarantulas difficult pets.

Next, you should look at all the tarantulas in the store. Some will be healthy and some will be sick. How will you know? Check to see if the tarantula is walking around in the tank. If it is, then it is probably healthy. Is the tarantula curled up in a corner with its legs tucked under its body? If the answer is yes, you do not want this spider.

A tarantula feeds on a cricket in its silk-lined burrow.

Tarantulas lie down like this when they are very sick. This spider will probably die soon.

Look inside the tank. Is there any water in there for the spider? Tarantulas need lots of water. They can live for weeks without food, but they will die very quickly without water. If there isn't water in the tank, you know that the spider is very thirsty. Its skin may also be very dry. If so, it will probably not live much longer. You do not want your pet to die as soon as you get it home. You want a pet that will live for many years.

You should also make sure the tarantula is not injured. Sometimes spiders get hurt when they are caught in the wild. Count its legs. It should have eight. It should also have two little **pedipalps** (PEH-dih-palps) in the front. These look like tiny arms. If any of these parts is missing, you should not buy the tarantula.

Some types of tarantulas make better pets than others. Many experts say it is best to get a pinktoe tarantula. The Chilean rose is another good choice. These are smaller tarantulas. They are quite easy to take care of. They also do not cost too much money to buy. Larger tarantulas are more expensive and also more difficult to take care of.

Many people like buying adult tarantulas because they are already grown. They will not need to be fed as often. They are already big and hairy.

On the other hand, some people like buying spiderlings, or babies. They like to watch the tarantulas grow and change. However, baby tarantulas are hard to find in a pet store. You will probably have to buy these on the Internet.

funFACTS

Tarantulas in the Amazon use the hairy pads on their feet to walk across water.

Once you have chosen your tarantula, you also need to buy a home for it. The pet store will have special cages or tanks for your new pet. Many people buy five-gallon aquariums. These tanks are made especially for fish and turtles. They make nice homes for tarantulas, too.

Home Sweet Home. This tarantula is making itself comfortable in the wood chips at the bottom of its new home.

Your pet tarantula will probably climb the walls of its new home just like this little fellow.

Tarantulas need very few things in their tanks. Don't put too much inside because then you won't be able to see the spider crawl around. You might want to sprinkle some wood chips in the bottom. This will give the spider something to burrow in and to lie on.

You definitely need a small container for water. Keep very little water in the container. If it is too deep, the spider might fall into it and drown.

Just like many animals, a tarantula will defend itself when it is threatened.

BRINGING YOUR SPIDER HOME

Tarantulas are easy to take care of. Adult tarantulas need to eat only every few days or maybe once a week. Their food is cheap, too! They eat crickets or flies. They like to kill their own food, so you will have to put the insects in the cage alive. Your parents may have to help you with this at first.

You will need to keep your tarantula in a warm place. The room should be 75 to 85 degrees Fahrenheit. Tarantulas also like dark places, so don't put your tarantula by a sunny window or under a lamp.

Tarantulas can dry out very easily. You should always keep a small container of water in the tank. This gives the spider something to drink. It also puts moisture in the air, which will help the spider stay healthy and live a long life.

Every few months, spiders **molt** (mohlt), or shed their **exoskeleton** (EK-soh-skeh-leh-tun). The exoskeleton is the hard outer layer of the spider. It is like a hard skin. Molting allows the soft insides of the spider to grow bigger. If your tarantula lies down on its back with its legs in the air, it is getting ready to molt.

This is a special time for the spider. Once the spider has crawled out of its exoskeleton, it starts to grow a new one. The spider doesn't eat during this time. You must make sure that there are no crickets or other insects in the tank. The spider's exoskeleton will be very soft for several days. The crickets can hurt the tarantula if they are in there before the tarantula has hardened.

fun FACTS

Tarantulas may have eight eyes, but they have poor eyesight.

Tarantulas are different from other pets. You can hold dogs and cats and play with them, but you should not do this with a tarantula. Why not? One reason is that the spider could get scared. It could jump out of your hands and fall onto the floor. This could really hurt the spider, and it could

This tarantula has just molted. Its new skin is really soft and fragile. Its old skin is in the background.

die. Another reason that you should not hold the tarantula is to protect yourself. Tarantulas don't bite very often, but they will if they get scared. They will put **venom** (VEH-num), or poison, in you if they bite. This could make you so sick, you would have to go to the hospital.

Tarantulas also have special hairs on their bellies. They can shoot out these hairs if they get scared. The hairs are covered with little sharp spines. If they get on your skin, they can make you itch. If they get in your eyes, you can go blind.

You should never put your face too close to a tarantula. You should also make sure you wash your hands very well after cleaning its tank. You also may want to wear gloves when handling anything that the spider has touched. This will make sure you don't get these special hairs on your skin or in your eyes.

A female tarantula in the wild. She guards her house just like a watchdog. No one will be getting into her burrow unless she says it's okay.

IS A TARANTULA THE PET FOR YOU?

Now you know all about tarantulas. What do you think about owning one? Would you like to have this animal as your pet?

Before you decide, you need to think about the good things and bad things about owning this animal. Tarantulas are not for everyone, but those who decide to get one are usually happy with their choice.

Think about your answers to these questions: Do you want a pet you can hold? Do you want a pet that is cuddly and playful? If so, you should not get a tarantula. On the other hand, do you want a pet that is easy to take care of? Do you want a pet that is different from almost everyone else's? If you said yes, maybe a tarantula is for you.

What do your parents think about this kind of pet? Do they think it is too dangerous? If they do, maybe you should tell them some of the neat things about tarantulas that you learned from this book. Tell them how easy they are to take care of. Let them know that they will not cost a lot of money to feed. Explain why they are not usually dangerous to humans.

You can also ask your parents to take you to the pet store to look at some tarantulas. Maybe if they talked to the pet store owner, they would find out that tarantulas are not so bad after all. There are also many other places where your parents can learn more about these animals. At the back of this book, they will find a list of places where they can learn more about tarantulas.

In the end, your parents will be the ones to decide if it is a good idea to get a tarantula. If they say no, you can always go to a zoo or a pet store to

It is not a good idea to hold a tarantula. It could fall and get hurt, or it might accidentally hurt you.

see these animals any time. Then, when you grow up to be an adult, you can get one of your own. If your parents say yes, then you are on your way to being an owner of nature's biggest spider. Be sure to follow the advice in this book, and your new pet will live a long and happy life.

BODY PARTS OF A TARANTULA

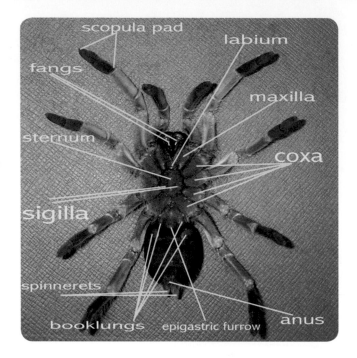

scopula pad
labium
fangs
maxilla
sternum
coxa
sigilla
spinnerets
booklungs   epigastric furrow   anus

scopula pads – Special pads on the spider's feet that allow it to walk on smooth surfaces such as glass.

labium – The lower part of the spider's mouth.

maxilla – The mouth part where the spider's teeth are located.

coxa – Part of the leg closest to the body.

anus – The opening where waste products come out of the body.

epigastric furrow – The opening where the eggs come out of the female spider.

booklungs – The organs that let the spider breathe.

spinnerets – The organs that spin the silk to make egg sacs and webs.

sigillum (plural: *sigilla*) – Part of the sternum where the muscles are attached inside the spider.

sternum – The central shield on the underside of the spider.

fangs – Sharp, hollow needle-like structures that contain a poison called venom.

Books and Articles

"A Bug's Life." *Kids Tribute.* Spring 2005.

Churchman, Deborah. "Tarantulas." *Ranger Rick.* March 1998.

Crosby, Alexander L. *Tarantulas, the Biggest Spiders.* New York: Walker, 1981.

LaBonte, Gail. *The Tarantula.* Minneapolis: Dillon Press, 1991.

Lambeth, Ellen. "Terror-ific Tarantulas!" *Ranger Rick.* February 2001.

Linn, Laura. "Spider Sleuths." *Scholastic News*—Edition 4. October 31, 2005.

Lund, Dale. *All About Tarantulas.* Neptune City, New Jersey: T.F.H. Publications, 1977.

Montgomery, Sy. *The Tarantula Scientist.* Boston: Houghton Mifflin, 2004.

Storad, Conrad J. *Tarantulas.* Minneapolis: Lerner Publications, 1998.

"Tarantula's Poison Might Be Harmful." *Weekly Reader*—*Edition 2.* September 20, 2002, p. 4.

Works Consulted

Atkinson, Ron. *Find-a-Spider Guide.* University of Southern Queensland. http://www.usq.edu.au/spider/info/glossary.htm

Chamberlin, Ralph V. *New American Tarantulas of the Family Aviculariidae.* Salt Lake City: University of Utah, 1940.

Dickerson, Justin. "Spiders Catch an Itsy-Bitsy Girl's Interest." *USA Today.* December 15, 2004.

Milius, Susan. "Meeting Danielle the Tarantula." *Science News.* February 9, 2002, p. 90.

"Taking Care of Unusual Pets." *Monkeyshines on Health & Science.* January 1999, pp. 37–38.

Spiders—Spiders Outside. Australian Museum. http://www.austmus.gov.au/spiders/toolkit/structure/outside.htm

Taylor, Pete. "Though Harmless to People, the Tarantula Inspires Both Passion and Terror." *National Wildlife.* June/July 2000, p. 16.

Web Addresses

American Tarantula Society: http://atshq.org

Tarantulas.com: http://www.tarantulas.com

Desert USA—Tarantulas: http://www.desertusa.com/july96/du_taran.html

Tarantulas on National Geographic: http://www.nationalgeographic.com/tarantulas/index2.html

arachnophobia (uh-RAK-noh-FOH-bee-ah)—extreme fear of spiders.

carnivores (CAR-nih-vorz)—animals that eat other animals.

egg sac (egg sak)—a special silk pouch spun by spiders to keep their eggs safe until they hatch.

exoskeleton (EK-soh-skeh-leh-tun)—the hard outer layer of some animals, including spiders.

pedipalps (PEH-dih-palps)—structures similar to arms located near the mouth of a spider.

molt (mohlt)—to shed entirely.

tarantulas (tuh-RAN-chuh-luhs)—extremely large, hairy spiders that live in both tropical and desert areas.

venom (VEH-nuhm)—a poison produced by snakes, spiders, certain insects, and other animals for killing prey.